With love to
Kathy — so happy
to have you read
my poems.

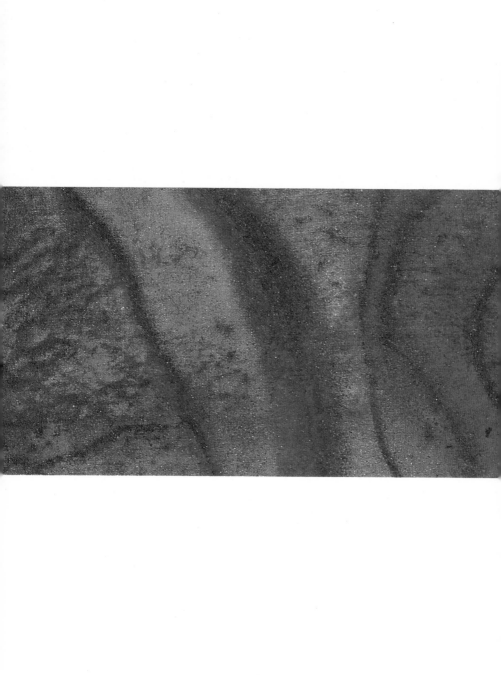

COBALT BLUE

Dorothy Raitt Lykes

Dorothy Raitt Lykes

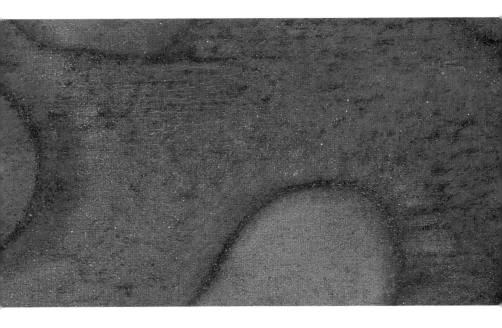

a sun lizard book

SUN/gemini Press
Tucson
1995

SUN/gemini Press publishes poets of Arizona and of the desert Southwest and, occasionally, of places farther afield.

SUN/gemini Press is a not-for-profit corporation.

SUN/gemini Press
P.O. Box 42170
Tucson, AZ 85733
520-299-1097

The cover painting, "Harlequin," an acrylic on canvas by David Andres, Tucson, is used with the permission of the artist and of Davis Dominguez Gallery, Tucson. "Harlequin" copyright 1994 by David Andres.

Library of Congress Cataloging-in-Publication Data

Lykes, Dorothy Raitt, 1923-
    Cobalt blue / Dorothy Raitt Lykes.
        p.   cm. -- (A sun lizard book)
    ISBN 0-933313-25-X (paperback) : $12.95. -- ISBN 0-933313-24-1
(trade hard) : $20.00. -- ISBN 0-933313-23-3 (special signed) :
$30.00
    1. Death--Poetry. 2. Widows--Poetry. I. Title. II. Series.
PS3562.Y37C6   1995
    811'.54--dc20
                                                            94-46346
                                                            CIP

ISBN 0-933313-25-X

The Poems

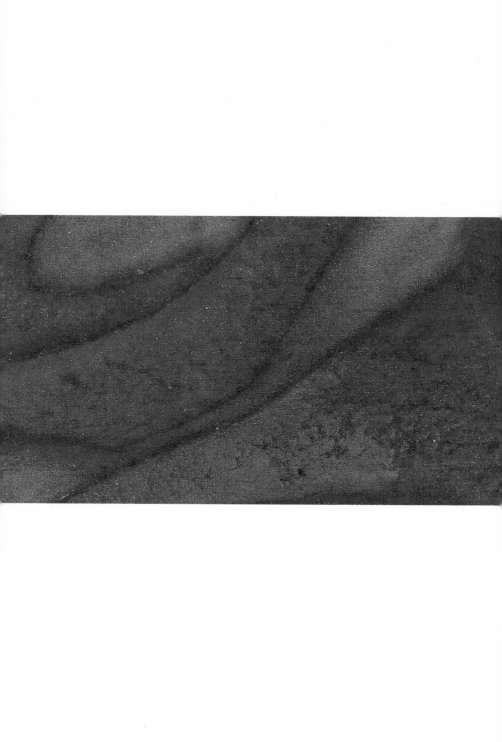

PART

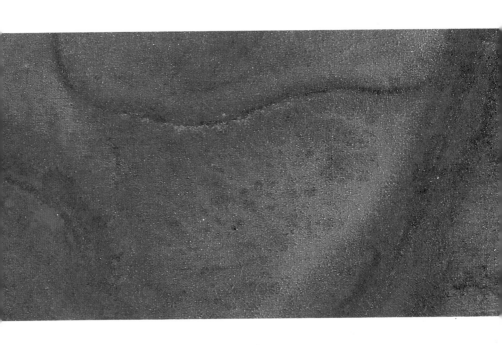

ONE

Our Marriage

You were the scent
of gardenias
on a spring night.
We danced
scuffing beach sand
under a full moon,
watched the slow roll
of ocean waves
pulling fog onto the land,
and tasted the ocean's brine

while overhead
the swoosh, swoosh
taffeta-rustle
of griffin wings.

Reminiscing

When I am with you
I dream myself to be
a night sky sparked
by more stars
than heaven holds.

With you I feel my spirit
lift beyond the bonds of earth.
I am Venus come alive
shedding pearls of water
into a sun-glinted pool.

My love fills the emptiness
of space with music,
leans against the wind
heralding the rising moon.

I understand how sunset
strokes colors
through the summer storm.
You give me back to myself
richer, and more blessed.

If I had dreamed
a perfect man, that man
would be exactly as you are.

Stability in Motion

The days we have left
I counted yesterday
as if each one were
a piece of gold.

I held them, played
with every one,
hoarded all together.
Some slipped, then all
fell through my fingers.

I shall not count them
again, but, instead, admire
each one that holds,
for me, even one minute
shared with you.

Living with Alzheimer's

You no longer hum the songs
I write for you.

You chew me to the marrowed-core
spit my teeth, my eyes
and bits of fat onto the sand.

Screeching gulls circle,
snatch fragments of flesh,
fight each other dropping scraps
for fish to seize.

You walk away along the shore
watching the sun's clean teeth
gnaw the horizon.

Four Months To Live
for my husband, Norman

He has become sweet
in the face of this thing.
Three times a day
I tell him to take his pills.
"I'll do that for you," he says.

Having lost his nouns
and trapped inside his head
he has trouble being a gentleman.

His sister sent him
his mother's piano
full of moisture, old rat nests,
and a rotten sound board.
A local piano maker
worked a year making
it better than new.

Norman sits at the piano
and doodles music,
the tones an abstract painting
with no background,
like Pollack drips,
as if his mother's spirit
is reaching for him
through the piano keys.

Our Vigil

The cancer consumes you.
You cling, without motion,
like a desert hawk gliding twilight thermals
before night forces him to crash-land
onto a darkening eucalyptus.

Once, making love, you said,
"If I step out of my skin
I will break into blossom."

Since your death I walk
alone at midnight and see the light
from the dead star,
Antares, no mass of fire
but light that holds its place
and glows — a blossom in the sky.

Mother's Final Lesson

As your nights
become sleepless
pockets of memory
rupture and surface

in your thoughts —
forgetting who we are
you call for Ray,
your younger brother,

gassed in World War I.
Your world becomes
a room with no sky.
You spiral on waves

of heat and near the end
your breathing slows
until life, a stone falling,
drops.

I drive alone
into a monsoon desert.
Cottonwoods beside
barbed wire fences

fling themselves as though
their backs break.
One hawk circles
on the storm's edge.

Permission

Lying beside you as midnight approaches
I feel your struggle to breathe.
Mouth open, each breath is a labor.
Earlier, you held every third breath
until the next one seemed in doubt.
Then a jerk and another intake of air.

I hold your hand, tell you to let go,
"I release you, release yourself."
You continue breathing, but softer
slower and softer, then nothing.

It is like the horizon on a foggy day
where I do not see the line
between the ocean and the sky.

I say, in disbelief, "You are gone,"
caress your taut cheek, kiss you again
and without knowing why run through
the house to turn on every light,
open every outside door wide,
and tune Tchaikovsky to full volume.

Two men come to take you
wearing dressy black suits. They pull
white plastic gloves from pockets
and roll you into a sheet.
As they carry you down the hall
to the gurney, one of your arms escapes
and flops with each step,

waving goodbye.

Norman's Death

In marriage your warmth
became part of me.
Held by your gravity
and bathed in your light
I began to see myself —

felt my rivers thaw
and flow through my forests
whistling wind songs.
I caressed the animals
sheltered there,

watched waves
pulverize my granite
on coastal headlands.

I walked deserts
filled with rain-splashed sage.

The glow of my sunrises
lasted throughout each day

until, in your midnight,
you extinguished
your light and taught me
the immensity of silence.

Unrelenting Memory

Your death shivered my world —
an earthquake —
house fronts pulled away —
slipped into streets —
leaving all of the nerves
of my daily life exposed

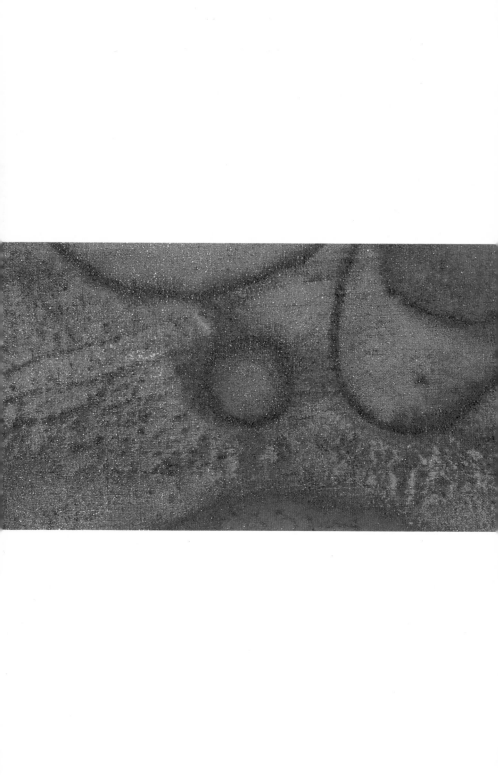

PART

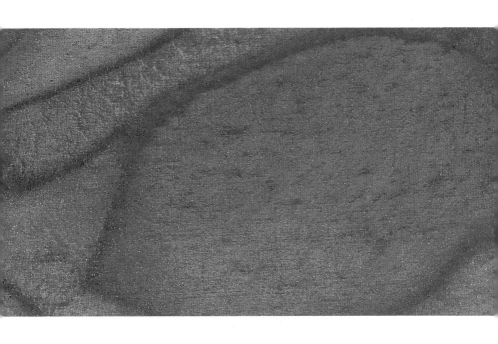

TWO

The Visitation

Last night I saw your silhouette watching me —
you stayed then faded and I remained
on the bed and worried, wondering
if you were in distress somewhere.

The night your breathing stopped
I rocked you and crooned,
reminding you how we listened
to the owls in our trees, calls in rising waves,
their wings beating in silence as they hunted.

As I held you your body drew warmth
from mine and I understood
death was not always cold.

Postmortem

I thought I was ready for your death,
for your release from suffering.
I propped you up to breathe,
and your fragile body felt as if
I would break you. After hours
of guttural breathing you were still.
It is not the way I planned.

Wait. I am not ready. I am not free.
Three weeks, and my body aches,
my shoulder, my stomach, and I shake.
I am climbing — the labor of climbing
steep granite stairs. Up and up.
The light is bright, white, hot.
My pulse throbs, red against red.

The stairs are cruel in their sharp edges,
steep into the sky. There is no railing.
My knees shake. I am afraid to look down,
wanting to sit so I will not fall.

☆

A rush of wind, a gentle voice,
You are not alone, have faith.
Step onto the thermal. Fly free.
I ease myself off the steps,
feel the fun, pure joy, of flying.
I spiral and loop into a cloud
where I become obscure to rest,
to pray, and realize I feel
your presence around me.

A Celebration of Hands

Work hands
calloused by brooms
and gardening tools,

uneven nails
mottled skin,
a surgeon's bone-deep

excavation inflamed
with pain and heat,
decades of

childhood accidents,
the pleasure
of holding your hand

through the night.
I remember when
my hands were never lonely.

Holding the Sun

Light as air I pirouette across city roofs.
Birds see my pleasure and stop flying
to walk across the tiles with me.
In my dance I feel the fun of touching space.

I remember the roar from the jungle
where monkeys romp upon grass.
They catch limbs, and swing over a stream.
Letting go, their splashes make circles
that grow wide and wider on the water.

I dive into the pond, look up through the surface
at the sun shimmering emerald light.
In the whirlpool I spin, close my arms
around myself, and feel the delirium of loving you.

Vancouver Island

Full-wall windows
surround my hotel bed
overlooking Victoria harbor.
I keep waking through the night
to watch the spectacle
of reflected city lights twisting
across the surface of the sea.

Earlier, swimming in a red tide,
I stretched to watch streams
of fluorescence outline my body
and waves crest with cold seafire.

I saw where lightning struck
the top of an ancient pine.
Circling down the bark
it cut a black gash into earth.

Two shafts of sunlight pierce
the rain forest of Western Redcedars,
light one strand of a spider web
suspended across the path.

I look up and see
cathedral trees touch sky
the grey-green of your eyes
when alive with fire.

Dream Magnet

Asking my memory to recall your face,
your voice, your smile one more time —
there is nothing of you

until, as a magnet separates
bits of iron from quartz,
a dream probes beneath the surface

drawing your face apart
from all others and I recognize
its gentle contours and smile lines.

Not the dream, itself,
but the way I feel upon waking
insulates me from this bleak day.

Lament

The lantern flame
is starved for air.
It flickers
the same way
I, deprived
of your love,
feel passion drain.
I drift into
flat monotones
of hours, pummeling
myself with remorse
for having failed
to keep you alive.

The Angel

While in a tailspin, I found the angel
I waited for. An angel who repeats
that life is a gift, an excitement
full of hope, who knows there are more suns
than the one in the sky, and told me
that a river finds its bed when stagnant waters
freshen and begin to flow.

I walk at night looking for my angel again.
I do not find him, but he is there because
inside my body my wounds are healing.
Fly, Angel, fly above the fog, fly
above the clouds, to where you can hear
everything at once. You have blessed my life.
You were with me at the perfect moment.

Working Through Grief

Floating, I listen to the ocean.
Water splashes in my eyes,
covers my mouth. Swimming
I hear a roar, look back —
a breaker above me curls
over its crest, crashes.
Sand scrubs my face,
my body tumbles.
I work to hold my breath.
Air. Air. My red bathing cap
churns in front of my face.
The wave recedes, I am on my knees
holding the bathing cap.
I gasp and know I am alive.

Awake, O North Wind

Recalling my marriage,
I know a kissed mouth
is renewed over and over,
like the moon in its cycle
coming to full light.

My emotions over my husband
are too large for weeping,
so I cry over other things —
The Song of Solomon,
"Many waters cannot quench love,
Neither can the floods drown it."

In meditation my blood
flowers into a flame of stars.
In that burning
poetry ignites.
I forge it for you.

The Confession

The moon rises full
with a golden haze.
I stand in the night
with my song, unable
to enter my empty house.
A mist begins to crawl

toward me across the grass
gathering everything
within itself as it deepens.
I never dreamed you
could be within reach.

I recite your name
over and over
like a psalm. The lyric
becomes an obsession.

Our talking goes on and on
as if there is nothing
better to do. I confuse
touch with desire and
feel thunder in my passion
too powerful to let you know.

Love, like a flame, flares up.

Learning Widowhood

No one to touch,
I lie awake,
press my arm
over my eyes
to shut out
the full moon
through the window.
Caught in half-
dream, a scarab
held in amber,
I am unable to
sleep. Hours pass.
My arm pushing
harder against
my eyes creates
a pinwheel, a confusion
of spinning lights.
"Be at peace," I beg.
I see blackness,
the unlit cavern
that is within me,
and hear my voice exclaim,
"I have the right
to be . . . ."
The cat pounces
onto the bed,
kneads my pillow
proclaiming time
to rise and give her food.

Carillon

Your remembered words
strike me, and my bells
sing out. No rhythm,
just bells. Some toll,
boom, some clang
exciting each other
to continue ringing
until my chance
for sleep has passed.

The Measure of What Remains

I control my walk
with a stomp, stomp,
designed to slow time
through days gone flat.
The lifetimes of people
I knew fade leaving
my children and
a few friends
to take my hands.

Wind blows past them
rushing my days along.
I resist, reach out . . . .

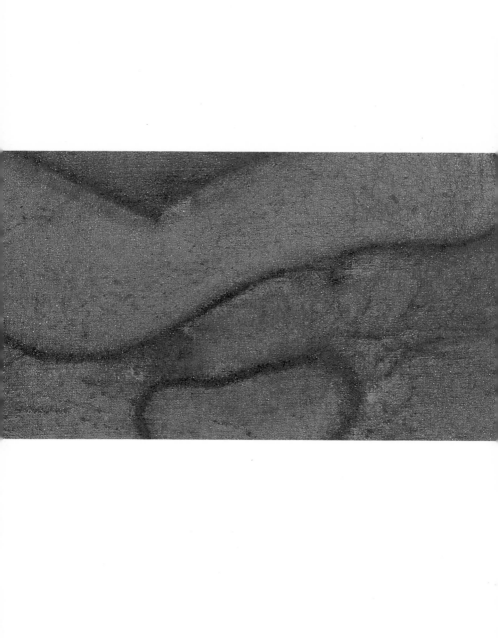

P ART

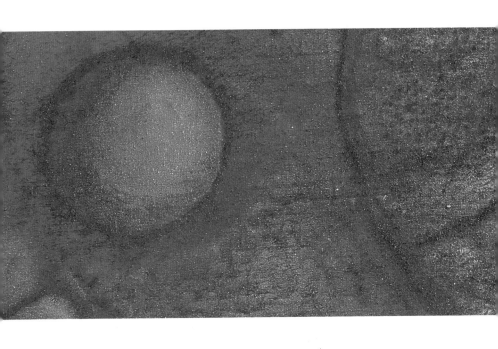

T HREE

The Yellow Dream

Blowing your cornet as dawn brightens
you climb ahead of me up granite boulders
until you approach the sun's face.
You reach out to touch it, and rock
it in your arms. Wild canaries sing.

You ask what I desire. Yellow roses
line a path that leads to the meadow.
In harmony we begin to sing.
Spirits come across the tall grass,
take your hand and lead you away.

You smile as you depart, and call goodbye.
Alone I take my yellow scarf and dance
through October's fragrant morning.
With leaps I dance to you, seated
beside the meadow, playing your cornet.

Condolence Call

You hold me
as you would
an injured child,
take my hands,
comforting the reality
of fears ahead
without a mate.

Your prayer sends
the fragrance of roses
through me. We steal
some time from time
to talk and listen
to the low tick,

the alto of a soft cello
plays in your voice.
Hearts drumming
in our clasped hands.

I tell you my storm
is thunderous,
the long roll of surf
pounding, then smoothing
sand as it slides
back into the sea.

Testimony

After we talk
I cannot silence
poems screaming
my insides.

You are the catalyst
that removes
the shell from seedlings
I want to share,
causing them
to explode on paper.

After we talk
I write and shiver
with the pleasure
of being understood.

Flight

A wild bird
should remember
picture windows,
arrow-diving hawks,
tree-shadow cats with gold leaf eyes.

Flying warm winter skies
I heard your song
and forgot.

Separations

When my husband died
you took my hand
to guide me through
thick, moist air
that blurred street lights,
obscured scenery.

Through months of
my fragile moods we met
to talk. I raised
my face to you,
a child hurrying home
in darkness, afraid
to find the house empty.

Yesterday, wind-stirred fog
parted. You stepped back
allowing me to stand alone
breathing clear, dry air.

The Crocuses Are Out Today

If I am the firmament
you are the dawn
casting out darkness,
a poem lingering.

You are the waves
against the shore,
pulverizing granite
into sand,

The mockingbird
repeating stolen songs.
If I am a garden
you are violets,

under their leaves
violins whispering
the Andante Cantabile.
If I am a prayer

you are the benediction,
the very moment
God himself
blesses everything.

Evoking Memory

Drumming my heart's pulse
my mouth blooms with blood
when you kiss me goodbye.
Your embrace allows my legs
to regain their strength.
The fragrance you wear
is caught by my blouse
and for hours afterwards
that odor is a ghost, haunting.

Two Melodies

His song
plucked
at her
nerves
as if she
were a harp,
setting the strings
vibrating
fortissimo.

Her harp's music
resounding
made her afraid
that her desire
might ask more
than he wished
to share.

Cobalt Blue

You sit beside me.
Taking my hand
you reach across
the immense darkness
since my husband's death.

Your eyes reveal your heart,
spirit filling you.
I have not felt this before.
My breath quickens.

You are a star falling
through my night
illuminating everything.

The Magician

Let me place my index finger
on your lips to see
if the magic I feel when
your lips touch mine
is always in your skin.

Seeing you, my pleasure
makes me smile and
I cannot help saying,
"I love you." Is it magic,
the feeling of lightning
that charges the air
leaving me singing
after you go?

Your disembodied voice
comes over phone wires
and fills me with words.
Where does it end?
Where does this begin?

Benediction

My world thickens
into slow motion.
All of my senses slide
toward my lips where
your lips are pressing.

You remove your lips,
touch mine again,
and twice more.
I look up and catch
your eyes watching.

My heart sings
while I pray,
do not ever let this
happen again.

Requirement

I do not
ask you
to match my love

for my love,
doubly kindled,
would melt
mountains,
boiling seas
until they
disappear.

Dorothy Raitt Lykes was born in Berkeley, California, in 1923, and was raised in a house — still standing — built by her parents. In 1944 she earned a BA at Pomona College.

She married and moved to Phoenix in the sixties with her husband and five children — including a set of twins; later she divorced, and married a man with four children — including a set of twins.

She has been a long-term continuing and independent student at Arizona State University. For many years she has taught at the Scottsdale Senior Center. And for twelve years she has attended the Santa Barbara Writers Conference, four times receiving the Distinguished Writer of Poetry award. "My dedication is always to the pursuit of learning the craft of writing poetry."

SUN/gemini Press
Tucson
1995

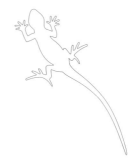

COBALT BLUE
Dorothy Raitt Lykes

Conversion of manuscript to *JANSON*, and all other pre-press, including text imaging, by Fabe Litho, Tucson.

Color separation by Hollis Digital Imaging, Tucson.

Printing by Fabe Litho, Tucson.

Binding by Roswell Bookbinding, Phoenix.

Photography of David Andres' painting by Steve Torregrossa, Tucson.

Book design by Clint Colby.

February - May 1995